One Brick Loose—Not Missing, But Who Cares?

iUniverse books may be ordered through booksellers or by contacting:

iUniverse
1663 Liberty Drive
Bloomington, IN 47403
www.iuniverse.com
1-800-Authors (1-800-288-4677)

ISBN: 978-1-4502-6064-0 (pbk)
ISBN: 978-1-4502-6066-4 (cloth)
ISBN: 978-1-4502-6065-7 (ebk)

Printed in the United States of America

iUniverse rev. date: 11/1/10

CONTENTS

Stories For My Children, Grandchildren and Great-Grandchildren

INTRODUCTION

I've had two husbands, five kids, two step-kids. Six dogs, three cats and two goldfish. The goldfish up and died, but the kids and dogs could swim. Got rid of one husband, and the second one and I are still dog paddling along.

I like dogs.

I suppose I might be a pain in the --- to one or possibly two people but on the whole most people seem to be able to tolerate me and I them. Being of sound mind and body at the present time there are many things I have to accept. I will never be thin again, my bra looks better lying on the bed than it does when I put it on, I will not be able to join the Air Force, I cannot be a nurse, I'll never bungee jump and even though my gallbladder is long gone, the gas is not.

I DO like dogs.

<u>Some</u> of the *1*st sentence statements are the <u>cause</u> of the *1*st *paragraph's* problems. Marrying young and producing children like an assembly line took care of being thin and the bra problem. Losing all my teeth at twenty-

two, due to calcium deficiency, a bladder uplift for sagging muscles, brown hair, now is the color of the week, and a hemorrhoidectomy (I like to blame that on the husbands and the kids) sort of finishes out the plan of destruction..

In my first book I reiterated some of the silly things (dumb) that I could remember and several of my friends said, "write a sequel.' They really are friends who want to see more of the trials and tribulations that have occurred within our family. You've heard the sayings "only one oar in the water"; "the light is on but nobody's home" and "one brick short of a load?" Well, I'm not short a brick but one or two might be loose.

Thank God, my husband, my kids and my friends don't mind my sharing our happenings. My philosophy is to live life with a certain amount of gusto, enjoy the good and accept the bad. It's called... LIFE.

BIDDING WITH NO BRAINS

When we moved to AZ from IL I tried to purchase several items with a western theme for decorations. Having several plant shelves in the house, I always had my eye open for things "western." We took a trip up to Oatman, AZ, a ghost town with wandering burros and history. While there I found a scrungy old pair of cowboy boots for $15.00. (The old hotel in that town is where Carole Lombard and Clark Gable spent their honeymoon so they say). On another trip to an antique store in Mesa I bought a beat up old brown cowboy hat ($5.00)... I was lucky to find a short ladder with only four rungs that looked like it was made to climb into an adobe cliff dwelling. It must have been for very short adobe dwellers or a one level adobe... Hey, this is great fun and I'm getting into it.

The coup de tat was at an auction. We had eaten out at a Mom & Pop café and when leaving noted there was an auction starting a few doors down. "Hey, maybe there is an old saddle or something there", sez I to hubby. "Let's go see". In my mind and pocketbook I am thinking I could pick up an old saddle for next to nothing. You know, twenty bucks or so. Forget that! Even old saddles go for beau coup and my pocketbook had zero coups so-- no way. However, they did have some horse tack that was going to be auctioned off. We took our seats bidding

Also, until the third son was born they all wore white polished (daily) shoes…enough was enough…I switched them to brown shoes.

Parental Love:

No one will ever love you or have faith in you like your Mom and Dad. Their love is unconditional no matter what you say, what you have done or what you plan to do. They might disagree with the choices but their devotion to you never waivers. It's something like the air you breathe: It's always there, sometimes it's so fresh, and sometimes it smells, sometimes it's not too clean but it is always there

Romantic Love:

Eventually, everyone finds someone special to care for, depend on, and share their lives with. In my case, I have been very fortunate to have the devotion of a man who took on the male parenting role of my four children when they were seven, eight, nine and ten… Can you imagine this for *forty-seven* years? Not only dealing with a very protective mother but sharing her life and her four children…then as if that was not enough, fathering another child with her until they were seven strong. This is love. (Or guts)

Perfect Love:

Above it all and looking down on us is God's love and He never gives up on us no matter how stupid we sometimes are or how many times we drop the ball. That is true love. It is from this example that all kinds of love are copied. Sometimes we forget and need to go back for a refresher course from Him. Don't forget to use all the love you can muster up for all the different types you need. Share the wealth.....

STILL FRIENDS?

We have been friends with this certain couple and have known them for about forty-five years. By this time you might say we know all the faux pas', eccentricities and traits of each other quite well. They were both educators before they retired; David was an insurance agent and I, a secretary/bookkeeper. . When they moved to our town they were inquiring about home and car insurance. David liked them right off the bat and invited them to come to our home that night. He called me and said, "By the way, I just met a nice couple and they are coming down tonight to visit with us." Since our lives have never been calm and we are always ready to meet new people, I was happy to welcome them. They brought their children and although they were a little bit younger than ours, they have grown up together.

The couple was reserved, quiet, and very mannerly. David and I were not exactly in that category. I think through the years we might have led them astray but not too far off the beaten bath. We seem to have, maybe by osmosis, picked up some of their reserve and them some of our weirdness. (By the way, when they went in to buy insurance they thought it was another company but liked David so well they bought anyway. Fred (fake name) just told us that last year.)

Many years ago none of us had ever seen an x-rated movie so we snuck into the late showing of some stupid movie. Jane (fake name) wore dark glasses so she wouldn't be recognized and we felt our way to our seats in the darkened theatre. Amidst many gasps, and "Oh, my gosh-es', we sat through most of it. At one point in the movie two women were smooching and you could have heard a pin drop. I said in a loud voice, "Jane, get your hand off my knee!" Poor Jane almost slid out of her seat and has never forgiven me.

Another time we were returning from a weekend in Chicago and had purchased rubber Halloween masks for the four of us. We wore them while playing cards in our rooms, drinking the furnished bubbly and laughing ourselves silly. We put them on when we stopped for gasoline on the way home and the occupants of the car next to us looked panic-stricken and ready to peel out of the station. We flipped up our masks and showed them we were not robbers or murderers…just two couples having fun. They visibly relaxed and smiled at us like "there are four loonies but we think they are harmless."

We have vacationed, celebrated holidays and all our children's special days together and they are welcomed as an appendage to our actual family. Too many tricks and jokes and too much laughter to go into….I'm sure you all have these types of friendships…

David and I each have male and female friends going back over sixty-five years. A male friend of David from his college days (fifty years ago) and his wife moved to AZ a few years ago. All four of us have been friends now for a long time…you know, the drop-in kind of friends, playing cards, laughing together, going out to eat and most important, the kind of friends that in a crisis you can depend on.

My Grandmother once said to me, "If you can even fill up one hand counting friends, you are extremely lucky. You are blessed if you can count even three". We all have many acquaintances but she was right….

friends are few and far between…we are lucky to have had them in our lives.

ODDITIES TO PONDER

1. Can anyone gargle with their mouth shut and their head tilted back? Also, must a person always close her eyes? Can anyone tilt their head back, open their eyes and stick their tongue out? (I just threw that one in to confuse you – I know you can)

2. Sometimes a person can flatulate so quietly that they are sure no one hears and they don't acknowledge a problem. Occasionally when that does occur, a loved one will be behind you or beside you and ask, "What was that?"

    You say, "What?"

    They say, "You must be deaf!"

3. Why does a person's breath always seem to smell worse in church? The singing seems to spread it around and then when you are back outside it doesn't smell so bad.

4. Why during a funeral service or a church service does your stomach decide to growl like two grizzly bears mating? This usually occurs when a point of the service is being made and everyone is quiet…..Many just smile and are relieved that it isn't them. Some turn and stare; some whisper and "eye-point" and dumb kids ask "What was that noise?" and look right at you… Little creeps! You look around also like "Who did that?"

5. Can anyone make a "snarl" with your lips on both sides?

6. I knew one girl who could put her own hand (fist) in her mouth. Do you know any?

7. Why do they call it a boxing ring when it is a square?

8. How come some people can wiggle their ears and others can't?

9. Why is it that cats seem to sense when a person would rather not be around them and tend to gravitate toward them? Rubbing them, seemingly to smile as they purr? The unimpressed person glowers, tries to ignore the cat and gently kick it away.......Big D is definitely a dog lover and our daughter's cat is in love with him. Will he weaken and succumb to Hermione's charm or will he remain tuff like John Wayne or Robert Mitchum? Only time will tell.... or a freshly dug hole in the yard.

10. Why is it…when you get up in the morning and feel like being cranky, sour and Poopy someone says "Hi" to you and you have to answer "Hi" back? You have to smile when you really would rather not see anyone.

    Crud!!! Ruins the whole day!

11. On another day you look like Frankenstein's bride when you step our the front door to get the paper – in your torn bathrobe, no slippers and the paper is at the other end of the porch and fourteen people go walking by on their morning constitutional and make comments… Good grief, people….sleep a little!

12. Another mind shattering discovery. Did you know plastic bag companies make special bags with perforations in them so that veggies can breathe? I didn't. After buying a new box of bags to divide up some "Friendship Bread" starter stuff for four neighbors, I was thoroughly disgusted when they were leaking all over counter and the bags were gooey on the outside. Now I know.….so do the four neighbors I gave

the bags to as the stuff leaked all over their front porches. Crud! Are you beginning to notice a pattern here that many of my good plans don't turn out too well? If there wasn't the "Crud" word, I would most likely be swearing like a trooper.

A TIGER SHOWS SOME
EXTRA STRIPES

By

Third Son, Randy

When I was a high school wrestler in the mid-1970, my folks used to unload their pent-up enthusiasm at my wrestling matches. Since I had 20/800 vision and did not wrestle with my glasses on, I could not see them in the stands but they always made their presence known. Both were blessed with a vocal volume control that slid to maximum at inopportune times. As I would shake hands with my opponent on the mat at the beginning of each wrestling match, both parental units would scream across the gymnasium at the top of their lungs, "Go get 'em, Tiger!" I imagined my opponent smirking at me as I gazed at the blurred image in front of me.

I usually wrestled at 15 pounds less than my off-season weight and was used to creative weight reduction methods – sleeping in plastic suits, sitting in saunas, running the bleachers during study periods, spitting into plastic cups during the bus trip to another school, etc. In my senior year I was competing in the 119 lbs. class and I was 5'11". Some friends call me "Coat Rack". Near the end of the season, I was tired of the weight loss regimen and became open to more creative short cuts.

Six days before the final conference tournament, I decided to take Ex-Lax for the first time. I waited and waited. Nothing happened during the week and I had to resort to my old methods to make weight by Saturday's weigh-in. So much for the short cut… After a wrestler successfully weighs in for a meet, he is allowed to eat throughout the day. I took advantage of this ritual and gorged on Twinkies, Little Debbie snacks, soda and numerous other items.

After three wrestling matches, I was set to wrestle for third place at the end of the day. The match was a close one. With thirty seconds remaining in the third and final period, the score was tied and my opponent had control of me. I needed an escape point to win. I quickly thrust myself upward and stood up. My opponent was still on his knees trying to hold onto me from behind with his face at my waist level. Unfortunately for him, during my effort to stand up, my body suddenly remembered that short cut I took earlier in the week. I am not sure if it was the gurgling and sputtering sound or the immediate odor that startled him, but he let go. The match ended. I was awarded an escape point and won the match. After the referee raised my hand in victory, I shuffled to the locker room.

Mother's note: He handed his wrestling uniform to me in a plastic bag and said he would ride on the bus. "Oh, No", sez I. "If we have to ride with it, so do you". He did.

OBSERVATIONS

Recently while at a gas station I saw an older gentleman (He could have been a jerk but I choose to think of him positively —as a gentleman) Anyway, this guy pulls up to an air tank, raises his trunk and takes out an evidently flat bicycle tire. I watch him intently turn the tire around and around seeing which side is the most flat and bouncing it on the ground to see where it needs the air. He finally picks a spot that evidently looks the flattest and reached for the air hose to fill the tire. He waits a few minutes, bounces the tire on all sides again to make sure it's level (?), throws it back in the trunk, slams down the trunk and drives off. Only at this point when I am laughing my head off at how stupid this guy is do I realize that he was looking for the valve stem, <u>not seeing which side was flat.</u> I was most happy that hubby was not there to witness my slightly wrong interpretation.

HOW <u>NOT</u> TO DO LAUNDRY
(FROM HUBBY'S POINT OF VIEW)

Recently I left home for a few days to visit family in the Midwest... Hubby stayed in AZ as he had some security work scheduled. Why is it that something you take for granted as a normal task always goes wrong and gets screwed up? Hubby has three pair of stone colored Docker slacks that he wears to work and for dress. One pair is older and getting just a tad frayed – One pair is about an inch too short so I ask him to wear them low on his hips to compensate and one pair is brand new, needs no ironing, keeps a crease and costs $43. Hubby went to work and got spots all over the pair he was wearing. Being conscientious, he decides to wash them rather than wait until I came home. Not only does he decide to wash them, he decides that bleach is needed to remove the spots. He has seen me using bleach on clothes before and assumed it was ok. Not to make the rest of the pair feel ignored, he puts the whole pair in pure Clorox! (I cringe just telling this as it makes me ill) After a few minutes he takes them out and rinses them in clear water. At this point he decides to call me for advice. He says the pants sort of disintegrated like cotton candy in his hands and perhaps he should have called first for a suggestion on removing the spots. Yes, it would have been nice.

You know the rest of this tale – it was not the slightly frayed pants or the inch too short pants that got disintegrated. No! It was the new $43 pants. He said he really liked those new pants and that is why he chose to wear them to work. I really liked them also – but I can't even use them as rags as how much dusting can you do with shreds of cotton? Scratch one pair of pants and save for another pair….and let me do the washing.

EVERYONE HAS A TWIN SOMEWHERE

Once while traveling through Texas, we stopped for a pit stop and to get a sandwich. It was a dusty, windblown off the road little Mom & Pop Café featuring Route 66 memorabilia and homemade pies. We sat down, a friendly waitress took our order, and a couple of customers made small talk with us. The homemade pie was fantastic. Even if you are only slightly hungry and they offer homemade pie, you shout, "OH, YEAHHHHHHHssss!" and order from the side of the menu where the pies are listed. I have been known to skip the meal and order three pieces of pie causing the waitress to stare a bit. (Got that from my Daddy – Always eat dessert first and if there is any room left, eat something healthy). Back to the story – I finished the pie and while hubby was paying the tab in the other room, I wandered around looking at the Route 66 things and John Deere toy equipment for sale. This was an old fashioned building with a window where the cook could pass food through to the waitress. I glanced in and a woman was wearing a blouse similar to mine. I smiled, she smiled. I waved a little bit and she waved a little bit. I looked at her and she looked so familiar. I looked more closely and saw the owners had filled the opening with a mirror and I was looking at myself! I tried to peek around to see if any of the customers had seen me and then I "slunk off" out the door in shame. Something like running into a window at a store that was so clean it looked like nothing was there and then hearing *boing* as your nose and face hit the glass. At this point you are also hoping no one is watching.

WHAT A BLAST!

For many of our youthful years there never seemed to be enough moola to waste on a Valentine's Dinner as there were seven mouths to feed and we needed to be wise when spending paychecks. However, after the kids grew up and we had a buck or two left in our pockets, David and I celebrated the event with an evening out and nice dinner on Valentine's Day.

This all changed seven years ago when neither of us remembered to make reservations for dinner anywhere. In Snowbird Heaven (in AZ) in February if one wants to eat out one either goes for dinner at 3:30-4:00 or is smart enough to make a reservation. Most of MN, MI, IA and many Canadians winter here and they all eat. Go figure!

Anyway, when there was no room anywhere fancy we stopped at the first place with a parking space as David was starving. Wendy's had many customers but room for the two of us. The next year we met our daughter Lori and her husband there, brought a rose and a candle for the table and made a romantic time of hamburgers and frosties. Each year after that we mentioned it at Monday coffee and invited any "tightwads" to join us requesting they bring a rose or a candle for their table. The third year sixteen showed up; the fourth year, twenty-two; the fifth year, forty-six; the sixth year, seventy-six and this year there were eighty-two in attendance. The open invitation to the TIGHTWARD VALENTINE'S PARTY read "Order your own, pay for your own and eat your own. David & Marilyn will furnish dessert (that's a shocker) and prizes."

We buy twenty to twenty-five gifts for the drawings such as plastic teeth, gag glasses and anything that we can find for umpteen for a buck. They are wrapped individually and put in a large red grab bag, numbered tickets given out and when your number is read, you may grab from the bag. "Let Me Call You Sweetheart" is sung by all with great fervor and laughter.

Wendy's helped with the decorations and donated $50 worth of cards ranging from $1.00-$5.00 for the drawing... We had a ball. Local TV station, Channel 3 came out and filmed it for the special segment this year. Any of us who were able to stay awake until 9:00 saw ourselves on the news.

Several of our children have been here through the last few years to play waitress, busboys/girls and help make the outing more bubbly. This year Dianne flew out from IL and Lori came over from Tempe and carried the brunt of the running and cleanup. All the retirees attending were very impressed with how pretty and how wonderful the girls were. Of course, we already knew that but we're prejudiced. The party was to start at 4:00; people started arriving at 3:30 and we finished cleaning up the place at 6:00. It was great – lots of laughter, friendship and nothing stronger than a Wendy's frostie to imbibe. The only casualties we have suffered was two years ago a lady drank her frostie too quickly and fell off the curb outside and twisted her ankle and a tooth from David's bridge fell out and we had to sort through the garbage for it .. BUT we found it and all was well.

Cheap but great fun!

VAN –DELIZE

I seem to have a continuing problem with vans with Minnesota license plates. Maybe it is all in my mind and maybe people from other states would also like to cause me difficulties but so far all I can complain about is Minnesota. Of course, during the winter one would think there is no one living in MN as there are so many snowbirds here from that state. The people I have met from there are all very nice and friendly. However, when they get behind the controls of their cars they "shift shape" or go through a metamorphism into D.A. (delightful angels-yeah right) drivers.

My first bad experience occurred a few years ago. A dark green van with Minnesota plates was driving in front of me. We came to a stoplight and we both wanted to turn left. The law abiding van driver waited until all oncoming traffic had passed while he inched toward the area to turn left. All traffic passed. The green Van continued to inch forward. When I say "inch," I mean this van couldn't have moved any more slowly with all four wheels off. I, of course, fumed at the crawl speed. Then, he makes it. The light turns red. I am in the intersection with a camera positioned on the pole flashing at me. A week or so later, I receive the ticket and my photo showing that the light had indeed changed. It was the green van's fault – not <u>mine.</u> The picture of me was not flattering either. Total cost: $125 and an eight hour driver's course.

Every time I pull into a shopping center I look for a safe place near the" return the cart" rack. When I return from shopping there are usually two vans, one on either side of me so I can't see to back out. One is invariably from MN. The other one is, of course a shorter van with an AZ plate (that's not too bad), Taking my life and car in my hands I move out backwards in spurts trying to see oncoming traffic. After making sure my windows are up so you can't hear my mumblings, I finally got out of that parking problem. This is not just once, you see – but has become a joke like there is no place to park their vans except beside my car!

A few days ago I was driving down the interstate minding the speed limit as I watched all the people who can't read drive eighty MPH pass me. I was in the right lane as I intended to turn off the highway in a couple of miles. I got within fifty feet of my turnoff and some D.A. (delightful angel) in a <u>white</u> MN van pulls quickly in front of me <u>in my lane</u> and cuts me off. Now I notice there is a disability plate on the van also. OK – so? The plate does not give you license to cut me off and make me slam on the brakes because you have a disability!

I also have a disability but they don't have special plates for "unique mental status". At the moment the score for who aggravates who more is…MN – 4, ME – 0! Just because I am originally from IL, that states proximity to MN does not give license for those drivers to treat me thusly. I object.

KNOCK-KNOCK
- ORANGE YOU GLAD?

I try to do at least two loads of wash every two days to keep up on clothing, sheets, towels, etc. Through the years I have cleaned several extra items as I did not check the pockets. I have washed licenses, credit cards, lots of money, lipstick (that didn't turn out too well), Hubby's cell phone, pocket knives, billfolds (with some of the above items in it). Today I washed a new item and it is now dirt free... When I pulled the clothes out of the dryer I found a sparkling clean <u>orange peel</u>, in fact three of them.

I had taken a dishtowel and an orange and sat in front of the TV and ate an orange like I do every day... Evidently I just wadded up the dishtowel and forgot the peelings and threw it in the washer to be washed the next day. I also found a feather (see 1st book for clarification) in front of the dryer but no baked chicken or dried bones appeared. It seems to be my lot in life to keep discovering feathers here and there with no reason why. But if you want advice on fruit peel washing, give me a ring. This might become the new "make your clothes smell citrusy" trend and just think you heard about here first!

CHEAP BUT CALMING

You know that bubble-wrap stuff that comes in packing boxes? It can be used for so many different things – We personally use them for gifts! They are really therapeutic when stress pops up. We send them on honeymoons with our kids, to kids away at college and if a person just wants to sit out under a tree and "pop" when troubled, go for it.. Many family fights have broken out between our kids because they feel someone else got more bubbles to pop than they did. I would not suggest them for plane trips, waiting for movies, or lectures or weddings to begin your popping experience as some people would not see the stress relieving value. In fact, they might get so up tight with their own stress at the poppings and you could be asked to leave the area. Some people are so inconsiderate! You might be in sort of Celebrity Company. You know, Elvis has left the building and so have you!

IT'S A BIRD – IT'S A PLANE – ITS SUPER BRUCE!

When we moved to AZ thirteen years ago, all our children were living in other states so this state was all new to them when they came to visit.

We have several TV stations so therefore there are several helicopters flying the skies watching for traffic, accidents, lost people, etc. On the news each day we would watch a copter pilot called Bruce. Spouse and I would get a kick out of seeing a copter and yelling "Hi, Bruce" just for the heck of it not knowing who was in the copter. …waving and trying to buffalo anyone who was with us that we indeed knew the pilot…

When our children came to visit they commented on the planes and copters in the air here (of course we also have an international airport and many small ones). I told them, "Oh, that one up there is just Bruce. I cannot hide from him – he shows up everywhere! He is <u>always</u> watching me no matter where I go and who comes to see me". I informed them that sometimes the copter even follows us when we are going out of state. I told them "he was probably hot for my bod" and obsessed with my beauty.

Our daughter looked shocked and said, "Are you kidding us or is this for real?"

About that time it had been announced that he and his wife were the parents of a new baby and I told my girls how happy I was for them – <u>but</u> he still keeps watch over me. I kept up the baloney until they got ready to leave and then said, "Gotcha".

This pilot is a nice looking young man with a beautiful wife and I think 2 children. I have <u>grandchildren </u>his age so of course, it was a big batch of it. I won't say it was a" lie" as I do not lie but I have been known to pull your leg if it was pullable.

My spouse was working security at the Phoenix Open and working in the media tent last year. The news teams were there and so was Bruce. Spouse told him this tale and he sent me home a golf ball with wings and his name in black ink. Whenever I get a live one to believe this tale, I pull out the golf ball and say, "Whatchathink this is –chopped liver?"

DAMN TOADS

I not only enjoy the antics of my own family – I live in a circle of twenty homes with an eclectic group of varied ages fifty-five and up and a variety of personalities. One special little blonde gal Donna (whom we love) lives next door and never fails to give me food for thought and fodder for my writing. We recently had the monsoon season here in AZ where it rains and blows and rains and blows and……. It leaves many memories each time such as trees down, wires down, roofs damaged, ditches flooded and <u>frogs</u>. Or maybe they are toads…whichever… they are seen all over our community in varying sizes from itsy bitsy to explosive size fatties that are rumored to be poisonous. It was told that one pet chewed on one of these and was dead within an hour... I cannot swear to this as it is hear say and <u>I</u> have no pets.

However, our little cutie has two poodles (Hershey and Cocoa – would you believe she is a chocoholic?) She is very protective of her two "babies" and ever vigilant for anything that might cause them pain or discomfort…..or death. While we were vacationing they were checking our house daily for any problems that might occur.

The scene:

Evening

The problem:

Donna with thongs on her feet..

The Bigger Problem:

When spotting a humongous frog on our driveway and wanting to make sure her babies don't eat any poisonous frogs, she STOMPED on the frog. Froggie slime oozed over her thong (on her foot) and between her toes and she runs yelling to her house and grabs the phone. She called a friend and screams hysterically "I just squished a frog with my foot and what do I do? Am I going to die in a half hour?"

Her friend, trying to squelch her giggles chokes out, "Just wash your foot and thong (on her foot) with some disinfectant".

Donna hopped off to the bathroom and cannot find any disinfectant to wash her foot with so---you improvise---right? She scrubbed with Zest and then grabbed a bottle of douche liquid and poured it between her toes and on her foot. Her foot was now "Garden Fresh" in case her husband develops a foot fetish. She's for real!

More....Our little Gal is involved with ceramics and has another story to add to her list of "I can't believe this". Ceramic class was told that vodka will cleanse the brushes and keep them soft and pliable. Our gal had an empty spray bottle that used to hold Citrus Shine to apply to her hairdo. She cajoled her hubby into giving her some of his less expensive vodka to pour into this bottle. She is so involved in many different projects that her equipment in craft-crap carry-all gets moved and left in various places. After working at home in her AZ room, she took her brushes and vodka bottle into the bathroom to clean at the sink. The brushes went back to her carry-all but the bottle stayed in the bathroom. For the next three days after shampooing and styling her hair she added the final touch of "shine" to her hair. She kept wondering why her hair kept frizzing up and was slightly sticky. The fourth day she realized that her hair follicles were all snockered and were fighting back the best they could from their inebriated state.

The bottle even had a tape on it spelling VODKA but always in a hurry, she did not remember this until the fourth day. Thus, the frizzy little gal lives to strive for perfection another day.

The day of her Mother's funeral she was using her Mom's bathroom to freshen up before leaving for the services. She grabbed the toothpaste and shortly got an invigorating jolt. She had used Icy hot instead of toothpaste. She did say that she had the freshest breath at the services...

ANOTHER JEWEL FROM THE NEIGHBORHOOD

Little M, (six houses down from us) has her share of kooky memories also. She entertained us with the hilarious tale of thriftiness. She squeezed several lemons, poured the juice into ice cube trays and when they were frozen, bagged them up in freezer bags for future use. Someone also told her that egg whites could be utilized the same way. She liked the idea and proceeded to do the same thing.

Several weeks later a friend dropped in for a chat and Little M offered her a refreshment of lemonade. Being oh so clever and thrifty she threw some cubes into a pitcher, added water/sugar and poured her friend some libation. The friend started to take a sip when she noticed the stringy gooky looking things in the glass and questioned what kind of lemonade was this. You got it.....Can't you just see and wonder what exactly was floating around and what it must have looked like? I just love my neighbors as they all make me look normal.

GOODIES BUT NOT DIAMONDS

Simple people have simple ways. It takes so little to make someone's day a bit brighter. To smile at someone – to say "Hi", to send surprise gift packages like the one we received today. Dianne and Dennie shipped us *something* a week ago and kept phoning every other day asking, "Did you get anything from UPS today?" I kept saying, "No, what is it I should be getting?" "Oh, just let me know when you get *something* ", daughter sez. Today we received a box about 12 x 12 x 15 and I couldn't wait to tear into it.

Bradford's Labor Day celebration used to be and evidently still is the day in Bradford (our IL home town of 700 strong). Parade of floats, tractors, fire engines, horses, cars, honor guard with the colors and upon occasion visiting bands excite the crowd of residents and former residents who have come back for the day. Singers and animals in Elsie Hodges Park people enjoying Terwilliger's bandstand/gazebo in the center…and contests are the flavor of the day. This is typical small town USA and great.

Dianne enclosed a picture from the local newspaper showing several different Competitions from frog jumping, antique cars, water fights, etc. One of these photos captures our immediate interest as it is probably the most important event for our family that day. Our great-grandson

Eric (with Grandpa Rick standing out in the crowd cheering him on) is competing valiantly in the water hose contest. The two competitors shown are in the three-four year old category and bedecked with goggles and holding garden hoses spraying forcefully a round ball to a certain location. Eric won this event with a trophy that looked taller than he was. Talk about thrilled!

Anyway, I digress…..

Back to the UPS box…After using a paring knife to cut through the protective tape I finally opened the box and saw multitude of plastic peanuts and a veritable gold mine of bubble wrap. Buried deep within in another plastic bag were five <u>IL tomatoe</u>s! You talk about happy…. we were overjoyed! They were green as all get out, not a bruise on them and although size wise (from 4" diameter to 2 ½ "diameter) they weren't whoppers, they were IL tomatoes. You talk about being happy as a pig in mud, we were!

They are now sitting in the kitchen window starting to fade from green to yellow/red and we sit and watch them. We haul up our kitchen chairs, grab bags of popcorn and WATCH…….We figure that in probably 2 days at least a couple of them will be ready. Oh, happy day – I've told you of the cardboard taste of these AZ tomatoes. We are sitting, watching and might I add, drooling????? It takes so little to make some people happy…..

DUMP TIME

In mid-summer 2008, I spent eight weeks with the chiropractor (not intimately but at least on his table) for a bad back/hip. Then I endured two weeks having and recuperating from stomach surgery. After that I rushed to IL for daughter-in-law Dawn, Rick and family. Dawn was fighting her last battle with cancer. Our son-in-law's sister also losing her battle with the same disease at the same time.

Our daughter Dianne and Dennie tied the knot on the 4th of July… so much for Independence Day for those two. We were happy for both of them and gave us a bit of cheer.

Before this we had spent a week in Clarksville, MO with the family and Dawn had made the trip. We each had a special time to spend with her and as I lay down on the bed beside her, we talked. She said, "You have been a wonderful mother-in-law". I thanked her profusely and stated that some people might not feel that way and feel I am an -------. In her own wry humor she whispered, "You DO have your moments". We collapsed into laughter and tears. What a dear soul and we all will miss her more than anyone could imagine.

After sixteen days of up and down emotions, we returned to AZ and arrived at our home at 9:00 P.M. to the rottenest, stinkiest, most putrid house I'd known… I KNOW it would have gotten a blue ribbon for that honor. The side by side refrigerator had kept running but the compressor had been out for several days and all the frozen meat, veggies, ice cream, ice cubes had dissolved into a brownish foul liquid with the stench permeating 3 rooms. After gagging, we breathed through our mouths (like changing a dirty diaper) and we proceeded to bag the content or sop up the liquid... We used Clorox on the fridge and the floor, sprayed Lysol spray and Febreze until my fingers got cramps, closed off three other rooms and hit the sack by 11:00. Last year we came home from vacation and our freezer had pooped out and all the food in it spoiled and we had to buy a new freezer. We were beginning to wonder what we have done to tick off the appliance gods.

Today they delivered a new refrigerator after the service man told us the compressor would only be working at 50% capacity from now until it died. So at the moment, we have a somewhat smelly kitchen, permanently bent spraying finger, no food in the fridge and a bank account that is barely breathing. Don't get the impression that the sun came out and we are all smiling at this point.

The monsoon season was upon us in Arizona, and our porch furniture had been blown off the porch after it had been pooped on by the birds, part of the siding had blown off and our outside watering system had popped a gasket during our absence so the water bill would be astronomical the following month. So other than dirty porch furniture, siding on the ground, kitchen slightly smelly, back/hip back in place, stomach surgery peachy dandy, the only serious thing we have truly suffered is the loss of our dear Dawnie. Everything else is <u>par for the course.</u> Oh, and by the way, two days later our big TV went out.... <u>PFTC</u>

OLD WIVES CURE

Recently Hubby found a couple of toenails with some fungus on them. Do not mistake this for….fungus of the bungus….or fungus of the monungus….this was on some toes.

Trusty Ol' Dr. McCullough immediately ran to her consult book (the internet) and put in "fungus, toes" and fungus toes, cures". Other than going to a podiatrist or a chiropodist (25¢ words) I felt home cures such as mustard plasters for chest congestion, egg whites to draw out boils, cucumbers for baggy eyes would work just as well if there <u>was</u> one for toe fungus.

Shazam! Sure nuf' – I read where vinegar & water solution OR Listerine and water solution could be used to soak feet in twice a day for a couple of weeks to eliminate the problem. Well, I didn't have much vinegar to choose from but did have a big bottle of Listerine. Mixing a batch of 1 to 2, finding a plastic bin large enough for size 14 feet, I proceeded with the cure.

The mixture can be re-used for a period of time then replenished. Herein lays the problem. I had the old fashioned Listerine (gold) to mix the first batch. After a few days, I needed to get a new stash of Listerine so off to Costco for the large economy size. It came 2 big bottles in a carrier. However, they <u>did not</u> have gold – they have the mint greenish/ blue bottles. No sweat! What's color got to do with it? Right?

When Hubby returned from his golf match I mixed up another batch and as he sat and rested, he also soaked his tootsies. I keep a big towel (you NEED big with 14's) available when the ½ hour soak is over. As the timer went off and the Dr. came back into the examination room (Living room in front of TV) Hubby removed his feet to dry them.

Good grief! I have turned him into a SMURF! His feet were BLUE! The soles and about an inch up all around were a beautiful robin's egg blue. Still playing doctor I instructed the patient to go in and wash his feet and dry them again. Well, dear friends – they were still BLUE! I didn't know whether to soak his feet in Clorox/water or live with the fact for a while that my Hubby has blue feet!

I love blue and it is my favorite color after yellow sooo......... It has been 3 weeks now living with a Smurf and they really are jolly!

ANY TEA WILL DO
(Maybe not orange pekoe)

Well, here I sit drinking orange juice and feeling old, dumpy, without makeup, liver spots and age spots seem to glow with visibility. In general, blah, bah humbug day.

Yesterday I noticed my hair had no shine to it. I suppose old age has something to do with that. I got out my VO5 and applied it and brushed my hair vigorously. My palms shone and the brush slipped out of my grip a couple of times and I sprayed a bit of canned hair gleam from the beautician and then - guess what? STILL NO SHINE! I remember Mom saying something about a vinegar rinse is good for the hair to get rid of buildup but I don't remember how much or what kind of vinegar. I dug out my book on helpful hints and found "brewed Lipton tea is good to make your hair shine". I didn't have any Lipton but had some generic stuff so I used two bags to a cup and popped it into the microwave. After two minutes I took out the cup with a hot pad (after burning a finger) and moved it to the shower stall to cool off.

An hour later (after a morning visit of gossip with my neighbor) I stepped into the shower and shampooed my locks. The tea had cooled and I poured it through my hair and rubbed it around. My hair felt dried and stiff and there were no instructions on what to do next so I sort of rinsed it off gingerly with water. I waited for it to dry naturally (as I don't blow dry) and picked it here and there to make it stand up a bit. I might have imagined it but I *think* I noticed a luster to my locks that hadn't been there.

While sitting down at the kitchen table I felt sure I noticed the sugar grains were sort of floating through the air gravitating toward my head and then the cream pitcher moved toward me also. Could the tea smell be wafting through the kitchen windows and into my neighborhood? I don't worry about the creamer as its empty – I use the gallon jug and it's in the fridge. All of a sudden an English "tweedy" looking couple rang the doorbell and asked where the wonderful aroma was coming from and when I said, "My head", they left abruptly. .Maybe if I had used Earl Grey tea they might have asked for a cup Maybe I have too much imagination?

Anyway I had refrigerated the used tea bags, pressed them under my eyes and lay down for 20 minutes. I applied makeup covering what imperfections I could and brightening the cheeks and eyes with <u>muted</u> colors (I don't want to be known as a hussy with tea in her hair), threw on a light shade of lipstick and sprayed on some Youth Dew (Oh yeah, I also gargled and brushed my teeth) No sense of downplaying the hussy bit with bad breath.

Whether wishful thinking or stubbornness I felt my hair was shining a bit more now. The strands of light brown, gray, blonde and white all seem to have a luster not there before. You suppose this stuff really works? I have to stop now as I have a call coming in from Queen Lizzie who wants to know what time I'll be serving tea.

BITS & PIECES OF A NUTTY WEEK

Life has its ups and downs and these things are expected. However, when all the downs come in a cluster, they tend to frustrate this poor old woman. It all started last Wednesday. David always plays golf with his cronies on Wed. mornings. The golf widows go out for breakfast at 7:50 to gossip and eat. I have not been going recently do to a problem walking. But--- last Wed. as I was sleeping soundly the phone rang. My neighbor inquired, "Are you going to breakfast this morning?" I quizzically say, "Today is Wednesday?"

Now I realize in a moment of clarity that David left early to play golf...so it was Wednesday. I also remembered a lady friend from Vegas had emailed me recently saying they would be in town and she would pick me up for the "Wild Women Breakfast" this morning. Her hubby would play golf with the guys. In a burst of Superwoman speed, I charged to the bathroom, and as the saying goes "SSS and shaved" (Now you might laugh here at the shave bit but face it ladies, those wild hairs start growing on your chin somewhere in the 60's). I even applied facial makeup (the whole 10 yards) to appear bright eyed and bushy tailed. I finished by 7:40 and sat by the front window awaiting my ride.

I sat by the front window at 7:45, at 7:50, 7:55, 8:00, 8:10 and finally got smart enough to go check the email she had written. It was for the

<u>following</u> Wed. I had sprung from bed, applied war paint and panting, and run to watch for <u>nothing</u>. Not only did I mess up there, I also had made an appt. for a haircut at 10:00 (forgetting about the golf and David not being able to drive me) You see, since my knee surgery I had not driven the car yet and the shop was about 5-6 miles. away.

The heck with it -I decided to gamble, drive slowly and hopefully no one would jump out in front of me as it is my right leg that has been repaired and it operates the brake and the gas pedal. The good Lord takes special interest in people with a bolt or two missing and sends special help to us. Not only did I drive, I also went grocery shopping for the 1st time in four weeks and realized half way though the hunt that my leg was giving out. I limped, scooted and dragged this old body to the checkout lane. I always pick the one that runs out of tape, operator goes on break, someone dumber than me forgot their items or didn't bring enough money so………I lean on the basket and wait and wait and wait (I am getting *very good* at waiting). By the time I made it home, my leg was throbbing and my temper was short. David didn't get home in time to help me unload so the same good neighbor that phoned me earlier came over and helped me carry $196.82 worth of food/junk in.

By the time David got home I had taken a Vicodin and was floating while he chewed me out for all of the things I wasn't supposed to be doing. With the Vicodin, all I could think of was "Rave on, Cat Poo – I'll cover you up". I know I shouldn't have thought that as he has been a wonderful nurse, housekeeper, laundry do-er, cook and driver for the past 4 weeks and has been terrific thru it all. His spirits were WAAAY up as he announced he shot an 86 today. He played lousy last week and was quitting golf. Of course, he says that about every 3rd week as he also has some crummy days…then he'll hit the longest drive or make the longest putt or break 90 and the sun comes out again for him. As I said life does have its ups and downs.

FATHERS AND DADDIES

My father (Mort Enos) passed away several years ago but the memories he left makes me smile to this day. I know we all tend to forget any of the incidents that were unpleasant and make our loved ones who have passed appear to be perfect in our memories. Why not? I have been so lucky – I have to think hard for unpleasant times Why dwell on the negative anyway? My "Daddy" to me remains 98% perfect and he <u>was</u>. I am 76 and until the day he died I still called him "Daddy." It was what I always called him and it always made him smile.

I remember racing him from the Bradford Drug Store corner to our house on N. Peoria St. about 1 ½ blocks. I was about fourteen and h was about thirty-six… He had been uptown playing cards with his cronies (he had been rained out of work) and I just got off the bus from detasseling corn (which had been rained out also). We were walking home for lunch and I said "I bet I can beatcha" – he took off and I took off and although I ran my little heart out, my Daddy beat me. Great Memory!

Once when I was younger he brought home a fox terrier puppy in his coat pocket. It's little head just peaking over the edge. Years later he brought home another little fox terrier puppy for Brother Jim… Butch and Zipper…..Daddy taught them all kinds of tricks and we loved them. Another time I had longed for a red-haired doll from Batton's Dept. Store - He came home with the doll for me, a fire truck for Jim and ...get this....a bag of peanuts for Mom. She, of course, knew of his plans and Okayed them. Once and I remember as it only happened once so it stuck in my mind – on a hot day he piled the four of us in the car and took us out to Eble's creek to swim and play. I believe we even took one of the dogs that day. You don't need to be rich to have rich memories.

Daddy always worked hard and it wasn't often that he took time to just goof off. He was a cat skinner (a caterpillar driver) and left each morning about 4:00 a.m. When he got home he showered, would read the paper and spend part of the evening either at the Old Park watching a ball game or sitting on the porch. He had to retire early to keep up his stamina. He never said "No" or "You shouldn't do that" but instead would talk all around the problem until you saw it his way.

About his age of sixty-three we met at the Club Lacon Restaurant/ Bowling Alley for Sunday dinner. I was in my mid-forties. We ate and then I bet him I could beat him at bowling. He hadn't bowled in many years and I was bowling league two times a week. We bet $1. The first ball he threw he fell down and got a gutter ball. Mom about had a fit for fear he would break something. He popped up and threw a perfect ball getting a spare. He proceeded to show me how to bowl and of course, beat me. I asked David for the $1 to pay him and David told me <u>he</u> didn't make the bet and it was my responsibility. The next day I mailed Daddy 100 pennies. It cost me much more to mail them but it was more fun. He was fun, funny, and dependable, loved his family and when they came along, his grandchildren and great- grandchildren. He was well liked as a fellow worker, card player, needler and joke player. When he was in his 80's Jim even got him to dress up for a Halloween party at his granddaughter's home. Cane and all he was a real "spook". David and I gave him his first birthday party ever when he was 55. Of course it had to be a surprise party or he wouldn't have come. He was also very shy believe it or not underneath all that humor. He stuttered as a boy and was laughed at a lot. He learned to make humor his protector so people would laugh with him... Not at him. What wonderful memories and how I was lucky to have him as my father. Everyone should be so lucky.

FECAL MATTER HAPPENS!

This title is in fact a true statement. There are some days when no matter how good you feel, how nice the weather is, what pleasant things you have planned ------feces happens!

My spouse has been suffering from back pain for several days – ranging from two to ten on a pain scale. It varied depending on ice packs, heating pads, Tylenol, Omega 3+ rubbed on back and assistance given by his attending spouse. Sporadic, <u>emphatic </u>salty words were <u>shouted,</u> uttered and whispered but to no avail. We ventured to our physician who enlightened us with: DUH...You have a back pain – there is a knot back there- maybe a chiropractic massage would help- take Tylenol and this muscle relaxer - etc. etc. etc. That was on Monday.

Tuesday, Wednesday, Thursday and Friday visits were made to the chiropractor at $30 a pop co-pay. While spouse is being worked on by chiropractor the fourth day, I make an errand run to return wrong color items to a store. Now this store was at Alma School Road and Southern – (to locals). To <u>my</u> family it is on the corner of "Grandma's Bank with the blue lights at night" – another description of location might be – to hell and back from the chiropractor's office (about 18-20 miles up the road a piece). I dropped off spouse for his treatment, proceeded the 18-20 miles, got out of the car and locked it and punched the button on the key chain to open the trunk. This is where the items to be returned were being kept. After retrieving said items and while in the process of slamming the trunk shut, the car keys slip out of my hand and fall inside the closing trunk. "Oh, Poop!" sez me. That and a few other choice words maybe…

Now what do I do? The store was to open at 10:00 – it was 9:58. Darn stores don't open until they absolutely <u>have to.</u> However, I did have my cell phone - but no phone book -. Light Bulb? Light Bulb! Call 411 Information and pay $1.75 to find out the police's number…try to find a pencil and paper to write down the number… call the police and the gal sez – "We don't go out and unlock cars anymore. You will have to find a locksmith". Bully, Bully – sounds like a fantastic idea! I plead with her to look in her phone book as the store is still not open and I do not have access to a phone book. She is gracious and gives me a number to call. I call and the fellow says 10 minutes and what is my cell number in case they need to reach me. I shake my head and state unequivocally. "I know my home phone number and my spouse's cell number but I DO NOT KNOW my own cell phone number". He tries to sound like I am not an imbecile and says, "Okay, where are you?" I give him directions and by then (10:08) the store manager had arrived and was opening the door. I am sweet as can be, get my items exchanged and ask for a chair so I may sit out in front (because of my advanced age) and await the locksmith. Since I am the only customer in the store and absolutely no one else is in the parking lot, they bring me out a chair on casters. Shortly thereafter, the locksmith arrives and within two seconds has the door unlocked. I can then press the door button to unlock the trunk and get my keys. He is very cordial as he hands me a bill for $50 and I hand him my bank card. Spouse will undoubtedly put the thumbscrews to me for punishment for this fiasco.

I head for the chiro's office knowing it is on Apache Trail but thinking I must first stop one street South at Broadway to return the last item I have in the car. I get close and remember the store is <u>not</u> on Broadway but back on Apache Trail. I say some choice words to me berating my intelligence and go back one block. I find the store, take care of my business and head out again for the chiro's office.

Spouse calls on the cell phone and sez, "Where are you? I am finished."

I answer sweetly, "I am on the way and will be there shortly". I drive a block and think; I am on the wrong street and will have to go a block north. As I am turning north I think again. Crud-- I am already on the right street. I turn around in a gas station, go back to the light and await a green light... After ½ of Arizona's population pass in front of me I finally get a green light. I drive like the devil is snapping at my heels, knowing he very well might be when I arrive at the chiro's office. I arrive and see my spouse is waiting outside.

I chirp, "Hi, Honey!"

He says, "What took you so long?"

I weakly murmur, "Well… I <u>didn't</u> have an accident".

He says, "Oh, no – what <u>did</u> happen?"

"Well……….."

His back didn't feel any better, my frazzled story didn't help and bank account was now $50 plus $30 less (for the chiro) than it was yesterday PLUS $1.75 charge will be coming on the cell phone bill for an information charge...

It is now Saturday...no chiro appts.... no returns to make and my spouse is still taking all the recommended ideas for helping with the pain. The pain in the bank account is not so easily cured either.

Fecal Matter Happens!

GROUNDS FOR DIVORCE

Well, if that doesn't take the cake!!! After forty-seven years of meals together, me fixing', him fixing', and both eaten', I got chewed out at breakfast this morning!

I had fixed bacon/eggs/juice/toast yesterday. (A good wife does these things, right?) Not wanting to send our cholesterol through the roof, I decided to fix juice/cereal/toast/fruit today. First of all, hubby dragged his way to the table *eventually* (he was cutting roasts in half for the freezer – there are just the two of us now instead of seven). Of course, the toast is like cardboard and even the butter didn't soften it but---He started out with a snarl and said, "How many pieces of toast did you fix for me?"

I, cowering in fright said, "*Three?*"

"How many did you fix for me yesterday?"

Sliding down on my knees for forgiveness I mumbled, "*Three.*"

"*How* many did you make today? "

"*Four*"

"How many did you eat?"

"One"

Holy cow thought I – what will he say now?

Then in a rumbling voice reminiscent of Charton Heston on the mountain, he spewed, "I only eat <u>three</u> pieces of toast when I have bacon and eggs. I eat <u>two</u> pieces of toast when I have cereal. Would you like me to put this buttered piece of cardboard back into the bread sack or throw it wastefully away?"

This question took only one nano-second for me to decide where he should put the extra piece of toast.

I then asked in <u>my</u> Charlene Heston voice, "After you shove it, do you want a divorce?"

He agreed that possibly this was not grounds for divorce if I attempted to remember from now on. I looked passive while thinking "Tomorrow he will either have half a loaf of toast with no cereal OR eggs…. or I will mistakenly make too much or too little and tell him to MAKE HIS OWN DAMN TOAST…. Or better yet, let's go to IHOP! (Always have Plan B and Plan C ready)

"YA'LL" FOR A WEEK

Southern belle, my… foot! I couldn't even muster up a small chime let alone a bell! We just spent a week in Hilton Head eatin' grits, drinkin' sweet tea, and hearin" "ya'll come back, ya hear?" The southern graciousness is always shown to us Yankees even though some of the rednecks would still like to blister our behinds with buckshot.

To start off with the plane leaving Phoenix had a flat tire after we had taxied out to the tarmac. No sweat – right? After we finally took off an hour later, the automatic thing-ama-jig that tells how many miles you have gone and how many to go and what the altitude is shows up. Zero Altitude!! We were cruising along but I figured we were only a few feet off the ground and the tire repairman must have been below us in his truck with another spare tire. We arrived safely – no more flats.

The price of the accommodations, food, clothing, entertainment somehow shattered the ambiance of first rate hospitality. However, the actual food, accommodations and entertainment were first rate. I like great food at low prices, superior accommodations at low prices and love a bargain wherever I can get one. I even went to a Thrift Shop on Hilton Head. Another shopper was heard saying "this outfit is almost Cape Cod-ish," I thought "well, la te da". I was looking for Bradford. Kewanee, Peoria –ish. The apparel thrift shop was definitely upscale thrift – lovely dresses, suits, fur capes (?), and used jewelry were not in my budget. Beautiful formal gowns marked down to $300-$600 that to me were like debutante type attire. I remember buying formal gowns from a thrift shop for our daughter to play dress up in and they were $3.00. Suppose I am no longer living in the real world??

We took a bus tour of Savannah, GA….saw the beautiful Catholic church that is on the tour, a couple of supposedly haunted houses, where our Girl Scout founder was born, lots of statues of soldiers on horses, a lady pushing a very nice baby stroller but instead of a baby, it was her little shih-tzu at the back of the stroller hung a small bird cage with a bird chirping away. Evidently this lovely lady wished her pets to enjoy the beautiful sunshine - but a bird cage? OK- now to the <u>really</u> important stuff…

There were candy kitchens hither and thon and I don't think I missed a one. The pralines of the South impress me much more than the genteelness. I thought I had died and gone to heaven. (My waistline definitely shows my love of sweets) Those little devils just melt in my mouth and I will eat until I'm sick, wait a while and then start eating them again.

I got back to the condo, phoned and ordered 3 pecan rolls and a lb. of pralines to be sent home. That was on Thursday and they said they would be at my door on Monday. The return trip was interesting also. David on the aisle seat, me on the middle and one of the world's largest men (but quite personable) was seated in the window seat. I tried to scrunch up as close as possible to David as the man's arms and legs were hanging over into my space.

I used the bathroom facilities half way home and when I returned he asked, "Do you think I would be able to get in there?" I hemmed and hawed and said, "Well, it was extremely tight getting in but as long as you don't start dancing in there, ……and be sure to lock the door".. He said, "Maybe if I can't get the door closed I could throw out a twenty and get lucky""... I thought, "You poor fool, stick to your mission and don't hold your breath on anything more than that" He eventually made the decision to make the trip. He got out of his seat - belly toward us. Although we offered to get up and let him out, he said not to as he could make it. I can't even go into that picture anymore and no one would print it anyway.

We got home yesterday (Sun) and I am waiting (not patiently) for the mail to come in today. With all the snowbirds coming back our expected mail time has been extended from 11:30 a.m. to up to 4:00 p.m. I figured I should take a lawn chair and camp out by the mail boxes just in case they come in early...

LONG LIVE THE SOUTH - <u>ERN</u> PRALINES!

HOW TO SHORTEN VISITORS STAYS

Unless your Mom was a really lousy cook, all of us remember what Mom made as the "best" and nothing ever tasted the same when it was made by others. Well, I have never pretended to be Julia Childs or Rachel Ray as cooking is not at the top of my "things I love to do" list. I seem to be more of my favorite comedienne Phyllis Diller type and throw an onion in the oven to bake if someone is coming. I love the way she thinks........

All our children expect <u>and get</u> tapioca pudding when they come to see old Mom & Dad or when Mom & Dad go to visit them. They phone each other to say "Mom made <u>me </u>a double batch or an excellent batch of tapioca and it was ready when I arrived". Rick prefers chocolate pudding and it was Dawn who loved the tapioca but that's something I didn't know for over 25 years.

Anyway, Randy and Sharon were coming from Indy for a visit this week. I had all the meals planned that I intended to cook, supplies purchased, some prepared ahead and then disaster came upon me. I <u>swear </u>I had a box of tapioca on hand to prepare for Randy. I swear! I looked, David looked, we both scoured all the hiding places that I have been known to put things but.....no box of tapioca. Randy and Sharon were to arrive at 3:00 Saturday. It was 10:00 in the morning, Saturday. I had frosted a cake, made a breakfast casserole for Sunday (in the fridge), David squeezed two quarts of fresh OJ, beef roast set out to thaw for a big Sunday dinner with all the trimmings and…no box of tapioca. What to do? What to do?

I did find a bag of REAL tapioca pearls that I purchased 3-4 years ago in some dumb health food store but of course, there was no recipe. I rushed to the computer and typed in tapioca pudding recipe. Got 4,000 – I chose the simplest one.

Instead of soaking the pearls for 5 minutes (as in instant), these were to soak for 55 minutes. Okay---fifty-five minutes later I followed the recipe and made a double batch so there would be plenty to spoil my 54 year old baby boy with.

At 3:00 they arrived – he asked "Where's my tapioca?"

"Here 'tis", sez I.

Sharon grabbed a spoon for the first test, took a big mouthful and turned away with both her cheeks bulging out with tapioca. She tried not to laugh, tried not to swallow and didn't know where to spit. I guess three-four year old tapioca *might* not get soft. After tasting it I must admit this bowl of motherly love was chuck full of what could have been tiny bits of gravel or slightly large grains of sand. This concoction would have been suitable for patching a driveway or hard road. Mom scores again!!! Knowing that his sister Dianne was coming in two weeks, he saran-wrapped the tapioca and put it in the freezer for her. This is true sibling devotion. Last year when he visited, he put books in her bed, saran-wrapped the toilet seat and put a note on the ceiling above the seat saying "Someone up here is watching you".

This time he saran-wrapped the seat in preparation for Sister Lori coming for the weekend. Good planning …However, we had a slight problem. My Spouse forgot about the saran wrap, didn't turn the light on and………..after bellowing "What the hell?"

He realized what the problem was. After mopping the floor and puncturing the saran wrap, he left the area in a snit... Unlike Elvis, he did not leave the building. After this "accident", I re-wrapped the seat with fresh saran wrap. The whole family is weird.....But back to my tapioca ...it usually is great....No, I am not kidding... usually <u>IT IS</u> great!

SPITEFUL SIBLINGS

We have five wonderful children – loving, happy, generous, kind and well liked by all who come in contact with them. I should say, all who come in contact with them except for their other siblings.

Since they were miniature people they have competed against each other for anything and everything. Example: When Dianne was four her three older brothers put her in the baby buggy and shoved it down a hill to see how fast it would go and if it would wreck – now they were five, six, and seven but------The hill they chose was called for whatever reason "the acid ditch hill". It had weeds, discarded junk, broken tree trunks and various obstacles that luckily the buggy muddled through. The buggy and Dianne ended up in one piece at the bottom of the "acid ditch". Needless to say, the three brothers got their bottoms blistered – I know, I know- today they should have to sit in time out or some other half-witted punishment. I am rotten and I spanked them with a yardstick. This yardstick saved my hands and arms for quite a while until the oldest boy put it across an arm chair and jumped in the middle of it splintering it into two shorter sticks. I then switched to a ping pong paddle which just fit their rears. Rather than go into long details of many of their "tricks" I will list some in short fashion:

1. #1 Rick took #3 Randy's toys and wouldn't give them back. Rick was full of it and Randy was the passive one of the group. This continued for some time and Mr. Passivity just floated through the pain of no toys until he could stand it no longer. Mr. Passivity, swinging left and right handed in a battering mode took the troublemaker through 2 rooms until he backed him against the wall. "Mom, Mom", called the troublemaker through his laughter. Randy got his toys back, asserted he was not always passive and Rick retired to his own toys.

2. #2 Mike decided to play a trick on Santa Claus and one Christmas Eve put an abnormal amount of salt in the milk left with the cookies for Santa... If he hadn't laughed so hard I would have never known which one did it but the twerp was so proud of himself, he bragged.

3. #2 Mike was always the one who went quietly past all other children pulling their hair and then of course, being long gone by the time they start screaming. Mr. Innocent was in another room entirely – innocent –for sure!

4. #5 Lori had an overstuffed bear that she called "Porky". She was about 2 or 3 and Mike was about 16. Doesn't seem fair, does it? No one in this group plays fair. The older ones used to throw couch pillows at her when she was learning to walk. This one time Mike grabbed Porky and gave it a pitch at Lori. She, of course, fell down laughing but when she looked at Porky, his stomach had ripped open and the stuffing was ready to fall out. Mike had to perform emergency surgery on Porky with black thread on the pink stomach. She cried, he sewed and the rest of us laughed.

Porky was around for several years to show his surgery scar and the preciseness of the surgeon.

5. Being short on money but long on family we devised many ways to have fun without spending money. With a stopwatch and great lungs, we had "hold your breath" contests for a while. Each kid would turn shades of red and white while trying to beat their sibling. I don't remember who won but at least it was quiet around there from one of them while the others tried to make the breath holder break and laugh. We also competed by throwing balloons into the top of lampshades for points – hey! May sound dumb but it didn't cost anything, no lamps were broken and we had a ball.

6. Dianne is a lot like her Mom and has difficulty with directions while driving. N, W, S, E is all neat letters but their significance is occasionally lost on the two of us. The three boys and Lori are all pretty sharp on what those letters mean but Dianne and me? Naaaaaa. Rick made a handmade direction finder for Dianne with arrows, letters, etc. to set on her dashboard. She finally bought a real one.

7. Another time Rick called her while she was driving somewhere and said he was from OnStar. He said she needed a tune-up on her motor as it was over due. He told her he knew her location and to _immediately_ locate a service station.

    Dianne panicked, called her husband Dennie and told him her sad tale.

    "Dianne" he said," You <u>do not have</u> OnStar in the car".

    "But they called and said......

    "Dianne... That was Rick"...

    Dead Silence...... but revenge was being planned.

8. At a later date, Dennie, Dianne and Rick were traveling to a nearby city to see a Reba McIntyre concert. Rick kept complaining he had a horrible headache so Dianne looked in her purse for Aleve or Advil and gave him two.

    A little later, she gasped and asked, "Did you take both of those pills?"

    Rick said, "Yes, why?"

    She replied in shock, "They were stool softeners!"!

    Rick stood in a long line at the restrooms when they got there "just in case" until Dianne told him the truth, "Gotcha – the pills were really for your headache". Priceless!

9. We have a family plaque that has a doghouse on one end and puppies with each kid's name on them at the other end. Each sibling tries to move another into the doghouse when they visit so that the next time the sibling visits, they will see it. Dianne took Randy's puppy and glued it into the doghouse. Randy came out to visit, pried his puppy loose and glued Dianne's puppy in the dog house.

10. The following year Randy was here first and put ET's picture in Dianne's frame of "Mom's Favorites". This last visit he replaced her pretty picture with a famous singer who is tattooed and drugged out to the max. She, in turn on her visit replaced his picture with an equally horrendous vampire's picture.

11. For many years after the kids were grown with families of their own, I would still remember them on Easter with a chocolate bunny. This became another family joke as these "kids" were now in their 40's. Really the only one still qualifying for a bunny from Mom was Lori who was in her 20's. Right? (That will cause an uproar)

One year I left a Chocolate Bunny for each of them and since they were not home, they most likely believed the Easter Bunny left them. Rick (in his 40's) found his and put it in the refrigerator to save... A few days later when returning from work, he went to retrieve his bunny and it was gone! A visitor's kid had the gall to open the fridge door, find the bunny and EAT IT! The parent of the culprit was visiting Dawn so Dawn got the dose of anger from Rick when he discovered the bunny bandit had struck. Dawn couldn't help but laugh but Rick was truly ready to stomp that kid. No one has the right to steal a 40 year old's bunny!

There have been many bunnies given between the siblings since we are no longer in IL but all are missing one ear, a nose, a foot or cheek. No one knows who left what where for whom. In 2010 Dianne bought a little bunny for Rick, ate the ears off and left it in his bathroom so he would find it that night after work. She was enjoying herself immensely until she reached her home and found on her kitchen counter – you guessed it….a HUGE BUNNY with 7" ears. However, this bunny had only one ear? Rick had been at her home while she was at his. Great minds think alike! This is an ongoing trick playing adventure that never ends Do other families have this same type of fun or are we just… different?…..However, it does make you wonder what this brood will think up next.

SOCKS I HAVE KNOWN

♫♪ WHERE HAVE ALL THEIR MATCHES GONE? ♫♪
♪ FAR, FAR, FROM HERE I FEAR ♪

MOTH KILLER

Some visitors are always welcome- some visitors are SOMETIMES welcome... and then there are those......

I don't know whether they have been sneaking in one at a time or in pairs but we are being visited by little brown moths who appear only one at a time so I don't know if the whole family is hiding or not. They appear when I pull open the shower curtain...when I open a blind... when I turn on a lamp....and only in the evenings are they mobile. I have spotted one in the upper corner of the bathroom, one behind the laundry room door and one sleeping in the corner of the kitchen ... up high so a shortie like me takes a swing at it with a flyswatter and misses. I take a swing at them with a rolled up newspaper, a magazine and a shoe but to no avail. Those little suckers are related to Superman as they are faster than a speeding bullet. This has been a contest for a few weeks and many little moths have met their maker. One, however, is still tormenting us. He is not welcome here and I am most anxious for his departure. To be politically correct I should say he/she or she/he as the gender is unknown. Big Daddy has asserted his power and height (after I find him the flyswatter). He swats and chases and when the moth hides in the folds of the drapes, BD dons Rambo gear complete with black face paint and bullet vests and quietly waits. He breathes quietly and slowly so as not to move the air....waiting for his prey to become complacent and feel safe to fly again. Silence hangs over our living room.

After a few seconds we notice a slight movement in the drape behind the couch. Perhaps it is just the fan blowing but then....it could be the dratted moth teasing the hunter. Rambo David springs into action armed with his lethal weapon (flyswatter) and corners the little monster. He takes one healthy swat and ...crapola, he misses! He swats like a madman several times in succession and although the moth has left several tracks on the walls, the final blow captures his essence and he feels the wrath of Rambo.

My hero! I can rest safely in my moth-less home. The victorious hunter struts around looking invincible and I quake to think that I should ever sprout wings, turn brown and hide in the drapes as no one invades our domicile when Rambo is in residence. .

Call McCullough Moth Killers if you have this problem – we will send you black face paint and a flyswatter!

DANGEROUS FAMILY TO CROSS

We have a three tiered metal flower arrangement on our front porch. Every spring turtle doves attempt to build a nest in the top basket. Every spring they start dragging twigs, leaves and debris in to build their nest. I open the door, they fly away and I drag all that stuff out and pitch it.

I don't like birds!

Two years ago I blew it and the dove laid an egg in there. She sat there each day and would fly across my path every time I opened the door. Finally she got used to me not doing anything so she sat there on the nest and stared "bird-eyed" at me. I didn't have the heart to ask her to leave her egg/baby as I too am a mother and we have feelings for our young...

The dumb egg finally hatched, the dumb bird popped out and flopped around for a few days and then one day, it was gone...Yay!

Last year they started building again. I again kept tearing it up and finally moved the whole metal stand elsewhere on the porch. I sprayed the top basket with Lysol; spray and Whoopee!! They finally quit trying and found another home. This spring they started building and I started throwing – three times...I finally moved the arrangement, sprayed the top with peroxide/water and then placed a white rag on top so they would get the message.

The next morning I came out and the dumb mother bird had left an egg on the white cloth. I griped, whined and started planning for next year on how to discourage homebuilders on my porch. Evidently this momma bird REALLY had to lay that egg and had no choice but she never came back. After four days, David pitched the egg. I threw away the rag and moved the stand back. Maybe she was saying "egg on you" just because she could.

Evidently others in our family are protecting their homes also as the following incident was sent to us from Son Randy:

"Last Sunday night after our Bible Study Group left, two home intruders entered our home. Just Sharon and I were there at the time. I heard them stirring in the house and armed myself to fend them off should they turn violent. I came across the first one and took a full swing at him. I missed and went down to my knees. Intense pain ensued after the encounter and I staggered to the couch. I found out later the next day that I had likely torn my rotator cuff in my right arm. He escaped.

The intruders were two entomological mutants of the horse fly species. My weapon of choice was a towel that I used to swing at the first intruder who happened to be clinging to the ceiling..

The MRI showed that I would need surgery which will be in two weeks and I will be carrying an underarm pillow, require therapy and will not have the full use of right arm for five to six months! The Dr. felt with proper therapy I should regain 80% of the use of my arm."

David kills moths. I destroy bird nests. Randy kills horse flies (or tries to). The moral is: Don't mess with this family if you know what's good for you …or them.

NOT EVERYTHING IS FUNNY

(Son Randy asked if I had advice or anything that could be of help to anyone. Doubtful that anyone would take it – I sure didn't- but here it is.)

Even though my parents were ordinary, average income people, they managed to make me feel like I was something special and loved unendingly. I was spoiled as much as they could afford and loved and encouraged with no end in sight.

Thus, when I began high school I felt I would be appreciated by all as much as my parents did. Boy! Was I wrong! No one cares for you like your parents.

As a young teenager I felt that I knew all the questions, all the answers and could control my future. Again…Boy! Was I wrong!

I picked out my future husband when I was 13 and a freshman. He was 18 and a senior. I was going to have this guy as my own… why? Because I wanted this picture to be as I wished. My parents, <u>my</u> friends and even some of <u>his</u> friends advised me against pursuing this relationship. Since I knew *everything,* I felt they must be wrong. We had a tumultuous relationship, going steady, me going steady and him not, breaking up, starting the whole rigmarole again with the same results;

the jealousy, the good times, the physical abuse, the good times, the mental abuse, the good times...How dumb can one person be?

I thought love was giving your all to a relationship. This I did... but somehow the return route got waylaid. After a 4 year off and on love affair, I graduated in May from high school and got married to him in November. Nothing changed. This is where you shake your head and think...."what could she be thinking?"

After four years and four beautiful babies I finally got the picture. I was not going to change and neither was he. He wanted to be everyone's lover and I wanted a picture book marriage with kids and a long future. Two entirely different roads...

For all young people who are in similar relationships, believe me, it never changes. No matter how many apologies for the straying, for the jealousy, for the black eyes, for the tears pledging "it will never happen again"...it does.... It never changes...

Thank the good Lord I had wonderful parents and a wonderful brother as when I finally got brave enough to make a move in the right direction, they were there to help and support me. I divorced my husband with three and 7/9 children. I was unable to even make a decision. All I was capable of doing was caring for my children and changing diapers.

My spirit finally started to mend and my strength came back. Don't think this happened overnight – it didn't. I spent a lot of time looking inward and healing and digesting what has occurred during the last 8 years. This is the point where you pick up your chin and march down a different road. Each day, each week, each month and each year I began to feel more like I was in control of my life. I finally realized I deserve better. It takes time but it finally becomes a reality.

I left my parents home two months after the last child was born and moved into government subsidized housing. My family wanted me to remain with them but it became important to clean up my own mess and take charge of my life again. I lived in the project for five years and finally got a job when the oldest child started kindergarten. I had an in-home babysitter for my children so they did not have to leave their comfort and safety zone. After five years, my parents put $1,000 down on a house that cost $4,000. (You have to think back as this was in the fifties) Now this wasn't the Taj Mahal but with paint, paper, hard work and friends that helped out, the kids and I turned it into a great home. It had a huge yard filled with flower beds that the previous retired owners had worked on. My Mom almost fainted when the kids made a racetrack for their bikes in the backyard and cut through most of the flower beds. But, hey... they were in our yard and so were most of the neighbors' children.

Seven years after the divorce I married again. Seven years after that we had a baby girl. I could not find the right kind of man at church as my church didn't believe in divorce. I could not find the right kind of man in a bar as 1) I don't drink and 2) I didn't think bars were a good place to find a fatherly type of example for my kids. I gave up the quest and gave it up to God. I asked Him if He wanted me to have a good man and a good father for my troupe, would he please deliver him to my door! Guess what? He did! An old school chum I had known for years came a knockin'. We have now been married for forty-seven years!

There is the right mate out there for each of us and the one we *deserve.* We all make and continue making bad decisions and have to pay the piper, but hang in there, look up and happiness could be right around the corner. Women don't change their basic ways and neither do men so don't plan on it. This is for all the young nitwits like I was who think they know it all and don't realize how little that is...think... think...think....

PONDERING ABOUT A THRU Z

Spouse David excelled in many sports while he attended Bradford High School (1950-1954). Give credit where credit is due is my motto. The class sizes ranged from thirty to thirty-five students so therefore lines were crossed over in several departments to fill a void. Although David had lots of heart, talent and strength in athletics, singing in the Mixed Chorus in school was really not his strong suit. He joined because many of his buddies joined and he wanted to be one of the gang. His body filled a void in the tall row. Singing with great heart (not so much talent) and strength he has pursued this love of singing to this day. While he has been singing in church, children have been known to look around to see where this sound was coming from only to be nudged by their parents to turn back around and not stare. However, at the end of the service they have also been known to cop a look at the song mutilator.

Daughter Lori is now taking a college course in Japanese and was practicing her vowels here the other day. She speaks French fluently and a spattering of Spanish – her father listens intently and then favors us with The Battle Hymn of the Republic and the Battle of New Orleans in "David-ese". His interpretation of all of these languages sound basically the same and we try to distinguish the language that he is crooning.

Three Blind Mice in English is thus far his best rendition but then that he has not tried it in Japanese. ....Lucky us!

There are definitely others in the family who might cause a double-take. Daughter Lori and I have been known to appear odd upon occasion to other people. Several years ago while waiting in a restaurant at the airport for our flight, the three of us sat and chatted. David got up to walk around and kill time but Lori and I occupied our time with a make believe dog that was supposedly under our table. We petted the dog, reprimanded the dog and laughed hysterically at his antics which of course we saw only in our minds. He got tangled in his leash with a table leg, wet on another customers chair leg and barked intermittently at children passing by. We exhausted all the tricks that dog could do before our plane finally took off. Yesterday Lori and I were sitting (again) in a restaurant waiting and she said very seriously, "I see dead people". I said, "Really? Do you see that dead dog under the table?" This, of course, opened a whole new vein of humorous ideas and we laughed ourselves silly.

I also remember impressing one of her grade school friends one day by taking a drive in the car to kill a boring afternoon. They said, "Where are we going?"

I said "I have no idea but I do not make left turns".

We drove all over town turning only right and going straight and it is simply amazing what a mess you can get into when you hit one way streets. They are both grown up now but still remember the fun of being stupid and nonsensical one afternoon. I am so glad we lived in a larger town (12,000) than Bradford (700) while taking this adventure but I'm sure it could be done in Bradford also if you just take the time to do something a bit silly to entertain a child. Of course, the gas was a lot cheaper when we took our drive.

None of these things are earth shattering news releases but just something to fill up space and maybe influence you to "Think Young". It's more fun! …..<u>or</u> don't think at all ….that works <u>sometimes</u> but not always……

STRESS AND I DON'T PLAY
WELL TOGETHER

Setting the Scene:

We have two cars in the driveway…one a 2000 Buick we haven't driven for several months due to its being non-licensed (costing $200+), needing $400+ to repair something under the hood, two tires a tad out of air., and the other a 2005 Buick that is in great shape. (This sounds a bit like deja' vu – cars and I don't seem to have good rapport) We are trying to economize by getting used to one car, the one that runs…

Our daughter who is getting ready for spinal surgery next week is staying with us. She is on powerful drugs due to pain so her car is at her apartment because she can't drive while "under the influence".

Spouse plays golf on Wednesday and it's his turn to pick up partner Jack. Therefore, our one working car is sitting in the golf club's parking lot. Here we go……

The Dr. phones our daughter stating she needs to take a second x-ray and ultra sound of her recent mammo. She must take them today as: they will be implanting metal in her back next week and will be unable to take pictures. They could do it three days from today but since she can't drive and we will be on a plane to IN in three days, that won't work. So, she said okey-dokey. They schedule her mammo at 1:30 and ultrasound at 2:45.

I call Spouse on his cell phone…hear it ringing on the table in our hallway. I know he can't hear it at the golf course ringing from here. I call Jack's wife to get Jack's cell phone number…She doesn't answer.…I call Motor Vehicle Division to get a license issued ($223) – can't get the license without an emission test. I get a three day permit ($1) to drive the car without license so no sweat, right? I am finally in control as I have solved all the problems. I try to start the car and it won't even turn over. …I cry…I cuss… I fume!

Plan B: I called Jerry (neighbor) and ask if he can jump the car, telling him my situation. He was afraid it would not start again when I got ready to come home. I call Donna (neighbor) to ask for a ride to the Dr.'s. At the same time she says yes, Jerry appears at the door with his van keys and says just take his van. I am not out of my bathrobe yet, my head is spinning, take a deep breath, thank Donna, thank Jerry, grab his keys and head for the shower.

Tell daughter to get her rear in gear as this show is now officially on the road. She showers…we jump in van and head twelve miles to Dr.'s clinic. My heart is going forty times faster than normal…The Daughter is concerned about additional pictures but assumes it's the same thing as last year. I assure her that it is most likely fibroid stuff like last time.

We arrive at the clinic and they take Daughter right in. I pull out my trusty novel and settle down for a three hour wait. You thought I was going to say "settle down for a good night's sleep and Santa fell out on my roof", didn't you? … Wrong! More deep breaths and heart rate is normal.…

Stress is sometimes too much trouble!

My Spouse got home and he went and purchased a new car battery for $128+. Jerry added air to tires and we headed for the emission control testing place.… $27+ and the car was purring, no emission problem, tires are up and other than a crunching noise when you turn the wheels, we're just putting along. Our patio sale was to be the following Saturday. We put a for sale sign on the car, had a Kelley Blue Book Evaluation for it and sold that sucker within two hours to a car dealer from IL who was spending winters in AZ and needed a second car for here. He was happy, Spouse was happy, I grabbed the check and was VERY HAPPY----I ran to the bank and deposited it before the ink was dry. No stressful days followed but Holy Cow, Andy, I'm getting too old for hurrying and worrying.

THINGS THAT SUCK
(Things I have failed at)

- Friendship bread
- First three turkeys I cooked were: 1) baked dry/no gravy, didn't know to take the giblets out), 2) baked ok, had gravy but again didn't take the giblets out; 3) baked turkey, good gravy, lied and said it had no giblets after I threw them in the garbage
- Christmas cookies (send girls to neighbor to learn how)
- Growing fingernails
- Tact
- Telling a lie
- Losing weight, (just because I can't. refuse candy, pie, cake, puddings, hamburgers, etc.)
- Many sewing projects (five-six still in big basket – if I can't finish it in three days, put it in the basket) I only sew for three days each year. I also only iron once a year so our ironed clothes still are really new each year.
- While using the electric mixer and blowing a fuse, forgetting to turn off the mixer before fixing the fuse. Cake mixings all over the wall, stove, toaster and me...

- My fingers on the piano – they used to hit the right notes
- Quit smoking for several reasons - (I REALLY enjoyed smoking) but –lungs getting in trouble, voice being lowered to Gravel Gertie status. My voice went from soprano to alto to tenor and was heading toward bass so I quit – cold turkey after thirty years. YEAHHHHH! It's been twenty years now and the results - I can't sing at all anymore, I gained 45 lbs. (I quit three times and gained fifteen lbs. each time), people usually say "May I help you, Sir?" when I talk on the telephone but on the good side – my breath doesn't smell like a dirty ashtray, I don't even want to sing anymore, my family loves me even if I'm "chubby" and my lungs are a pretty pink and healthy. (I still would like a cigarette once in a while but don't dare….okay – so beat me.

Time to Stop Sharing

I was seventy-six last March so possibly I should consider this might be my last endeavor at writing weird happenings in our family. After all, what else could possibly occur that has not been mentioned and laughed at? The Editor of my first book said I sounded so self-deprecating. I tried to tell him my sense of humor encompasses all the good things that happen, all the funny things that happen and all the dumb things that most people don't talk about let along write about. I am a very happy individual, love life, and love to laugh, love my family dearly and enjoy my friends to the utmost.

I have enjoyed and am enjoying every minute of my encounter with life – the good AND the bad. Believe me, there are so many more good things than bad and I choose to remember the happy times. David and

I have been married for almost 48 years and are still speaking to each other.

I have published one book and poetry previously and have written several children's' stories. The stories at the end of this book are for my children, my grandchildren, my great-grandchildren and whoever else wants to read them.

I hope you enjoy my book and can laugh at the dumb things that have happened to me and most likely to you or someone you know. It is so much easier than getting caught up in feeling bad, dumb or insignificant. I might not ROAR as loud as I used to but I AM WOMAN!

STORIES
FOR MY CHILDREN,
GRANDCHILDREN AND
GREAT-GRANDCHILDREN

AND THEN IT HAPPENED

This was the day that Lori Burns had been holding her breath for. August 27, 1961… the day of the party! She had lived in Bradford for only three months and had not become friends with any children her age. Lori's family was poor in terms of money, but rich with love. Her mother and father worked very hard. Her father worked at Gorman lumber company and her mother worked three days a week at the Spic & Span dry cleaners.

Lori told her mother about the Get Ready for School party at the church. She hoped to go and maybe meet some girls to chum with. Mrs. Burns stretched their meager funds to buy material for a new dress for her daughter.

The day finally arrived. A new dress was a novelty for Lori and shi was thrilled beyond words as she twirled in front of the mirror. Her eyes sparkled like snowflakes through sunshine… Her mother even let her add a touch of lipstick, but just a touch as Lori was only eleven. She left her home and walked quickly, almost skipping, towards the church on Elm Street. Lori smiled at the world as she went through the business area.

And then it happened!

Tom Loring, 34, had been unemployed for the past six months and was full of anticipation for his meeting today. His wife had laundered his best white shirt, pressed his only suit and he had shined his best shoes. He was to meet Mr. Johnson at one o'clock in the restaurant downtown to interview for a possible job with Johnson's company. Tom was almost sick with nervousness. Their funds were at rock bottom. Would this be his lucky day? He kissed his wife goodbye, threw back his shoulders and walked out the door to meet Mr. Johnson. With any luck maybe he would be starting a new job soon. Tom walked the several blocks quickly and then took a deep breath before turning into Garren's restaurant.

And then it happened!

Rhonda Grunloh was all nerves waiting for this day. The letter from her dear friend Dianne had arrived three weeks ago. They had not seen each other since 1949. The two best friends had corresponded through the years sharing news of children and grandchildren and many photos but it's just not the same as in person.

Dianne had married twenty years ago and had left with her new husband to travel abroad and live a whole new life. She had been widowed last year and had come back home to the small town of Bradford yesterday. Rhonda had loved her friend and had always envied Dianne's grace and beauty. Why Dianne had chosen Rhonda as her best friend, Rhonda could never figure out. Rhonda was a lovely girl and a lovely woman but she had always felt in awe of her friend's accomplishments in life. They were to meet at Garrens for lunch.

Rhonda wore her navy silk dress and topped off her now white hair with a jaunty navy and white straw hat. She looked terrific but felt she would never come up to Dianne's natural beauty... Rhonda had taken a taxi to the restaurant. She asked the driver let her off at the corner so she could adjust herself one more time in the reflection of the store windows before proceeding toward Garren's door.

<u>And then it happened!</u>

Randy had great hopes that today would be a big day for selling his quarts of wild raspberries. He had gotten out of bed at 4:30 this morning to head for the railroad tracks and the patch of wild berries. He had picked twenty quarts, ten more than usual. He hoped he would make enough today to pay his cousin off for a bicycle he was going to buy from him.

He had stopped at Dorgan's for a coke and was pulling his wagon and slurping on his coke. Boy, it would sure make all his berry picking work mean so much if he had a bicycle to show for all his labor. Maybe by tomorrow he would be riding on his new bicycle He was passing Garrens.

<u>And then it happened!</u>

Rick and Mike were best friends and had been since they started kindergarten. Both twelve now, they lived across the street from each other. They had read comic books together, fought imaginary wars, played cowboys, and were inseparable. They were playing a game at Rick's house when Rick's Mom came in. She said, "I am running late and need to take your sister to her piano lesson. I'll be back in about an hour." She asked the boys to put the two bags of groceries away. They agreed and she and Sharon dashed out the door.

The boys put away the cereal, milk, and canned goods. As they started to put the flour in the canister, they dropped the sack on the floor. Flour flew all over the counter, the floor <u>and</u> the boys. The circles around their eyes were the only dark spots on them. They laughed, as only children can, until they could laugh no more.

They pooled what money they had and ran to the grocery store. They bought another five pound bag of flour to fill Rick's Mom's canister. By now a great plan had been thought of. They scooped up the flour on the floor into five paper lunch bags and headed toward town. They decided the most strategic position for dropping their flour bombs would be the top of the second story of the building that housed the restaurant. They avoided anyone who might recognize them and snuck stealthily up the stairs to the roof. They waited. Along came a girl in a fancy dress. They dropped the first bag dead center. The flour puffed all over her head, face and dress. She was stunned, starting crying and felt utterly humiliated. She ran all the way back home to her Mother's arms. The tears made many streaks on her floured face. The beauty and thrill of her new dress was shattered.

The boys waited…soon a young man in an ill-fitting suit approached the restaurant. They tossed another of their bombs. The bag's contents blinded him momentarily. His flour-covered suit was a total disaster and his shoes were no longer shiny.

His appointment was in five minutes. There was no way he could clean himself up in time and his eyes were not focusing quite right yet. Embarrassed, but having no choice but to go in and explain to Mr. Johnson, he did so. He wondered "What have I done to deserve this?"

Rick and Mike congratulated one another with high five's on their successful attack before spying their next victim. "Hey, look…There's an old lady. Maybe she'll come this way," Rick said. Rhonda approached the door of Garrens. A bag of flour exploded at her feet. The flour covered her shoes, stockings and hem of her dress. After a moment of shock, she slowly entered the restaurant. Mr. Loring rose immediately from his table to offer his assistance. He asked, "Will someone please call Gilly (the town cop) before someone is seriously hurt and find out what is going on?" He tried to assist Rhonda (Mrs. Grunloh) in brushing off the flour.

Up on the roof Rick and Mike still had two bags left. They decided to drop them on Randy who was walking below them pulling a wagon full of berries. The flour bags definitely hit their mark and many berries were squashed and covered in flour. Randy felt sick at the sight. After all his work and now he would not be able to pay for his bike. His anger began to replace his sick feeling...

Rick and Mike were pleased with their afternoon's shenanigans and decided to call it quits. As they started down the stairs, the icy cold voice of Gilly froze them in their tracks. He ordered them to come down immediately. They were taken to the station and held until their parents and Gilly could determine what to do with them.

After reading an account of the flour caper in the paper the next day, several of Lori's classmates-to-be went to see her. Some went to her home because they were curious but most out of the girls went to offer their friendship. Lori relished the attention.

Mr. Loring was offered a job because Mr. Johnson was impressed by Loring's compassionate display and quick thinking actions at the restaurant. Dianne hugged her old friend Rhonda and began to chuckle. Rhonda, seeing the humor, giggled and said, "I'd walk through anything to see you again." Randy, the young entrepreneur, received twenty free quarts of berries a week for as long as the wild bushes produced that summer, courtesy of his two new pickers, Mike and Rick.

The two pranksters were ordered to pay $1.50 each a week to Randy for the next two months from the generosity of their allowances. The culprits were each sentenced to pay for the cleaning bills of Lori, Mr. Loring and Mrs. Grunloh. This also came from their weekly allowances.

Other than the berry picking, the parents made sure the boys had no contact for nearly three months.

A decade later, two young marines, fresh from boot camp, got off the bus in Bradford. They looked sharp in their dress uniforms. Famished, they immediately headed for Garrens. Rick and Mike checked each other out to make sure they looked perfect. Yup, uniforms neat and shoes shining, they started for the door of the restaurant.

And then it happened!

JAKE AND THE MUDPUDDLE

Oozy lay there in the sun. It had rained very hard for the past two days. People avoided him, ignored him, stepped over him and yelled to others to "Watch out" for him. None of this was his fault. What if he was slimy, mucky and sticky? It wasn't his choice to be this way. He was normally just a dip on the dirt path. That is, until it rained. He then filled up with water, got soft and squishy and nobody wanted to come close to him or walk on him until he dried out. He was so lonely.

Jake was a six year old typical boy. He was full of zip, extremely curious and had been known to find trouble without looking very hard... His friends and sister called him Jake. His parents did too most of the time. When they were upset with him about some trouble he found himself in, they called him Jacob. If it was BIG TROUBLE, it was worth a Jacob Andrew. It wasn't that he was a *bad* boy, just six years old and curious.

Mother asked Brooke, Jake's 12 year old sister to go to the store for her. She said," Brooke, I need bread and milk for lunch and would appreciate it if you would take Jake along for the walk."

"Oh, Mom, <u>why </u>do I have to take him? (She always referred to him as if he were a bug) He asks too many questions and takes too long to get anywhere,"

"Because I asked you to," said Mother. "Jake needs to get out a little and learn how to go to the store for me. He can carry the bread home and you can carry the milk".

"Right," and Brooke, "and drive me nuts in the meantime. Come on, Twerp: let's hit the trail for the store..."

"How old were you when you got to go to the store alone?" "How come the sidewalk has so many cracks in it and how come you don't step on any of them?" "Why do girls walk so fast?" Jake kept it up until Brooke turned to take a shortcut through the park. He then took a breath.

"Wow, did you see that bird's nest? I wonder if the birds just flew away when the nest fell on the ground." The new scenery started a whole new series of questions. "Wow, look at this' and 'Wow, look at that'" until they came upon a big mud puddle.

Jake stared in awe at the puddle. It was a doozy of an oozy puddle.

Brooke said, "Come on, Jake... just walk around it and <u>don't</u> get near it, Mom will skin both of us if you get muddy."

Jake again uttered, "Wow." Oozy saw Jake and knew that he might have a friend in this boy.

Oozy said, "She called you Jake. My name is Oozy. You can come a little closer. I won't hurt you."

Jake took a couple of steps to the edge of the puddle, squatted down on his haunches and stared. "You are a whopper of a puddle," said Jake.

Oozy said, "Yep, I'm one of the best this year so far. You should feel how soft and warm my mud is at the middle."

Jake stared and was tempted to step forward onto the edge of Oozy when Brooke called. "Jake, come on. Quit fooling around. We have to get to the store and get the stuff home to Mom."

Oozy could tell that Jake was going to walk around him and leave him as everyone else had. He immediately felt sad. "Go ahead, Jake. Maybe I'll see you around some time."

Jake whispered, "I'll come back tomorrow and we will talk some more. See ya."

The next day the sun rose slowly in the sky. By noon it was a full blown hot day with dazzling sunshine. Oozy's size was shrinking around the edge. He knew if this weather kept up, he would dry up soon into a patch of dirt. He listened to the usual banter of the kids shouting, "Stay away from the mud puddle', 'that stuff really looks icky', and 'I think that mess is going to dry out in a couple of days." Around mid day he looked up and saw Jake. Jake was again squatting down looking into the center of his puddle

"Do you have any fish in there?" he asked. "Is it warm in the deepest part" "How <u>deep</u> are you?" and "Gee, you look smaller than yesterday."

Oozy replied in a smaller voice than yesterday, "Well, howdy Jake. Glad to have some company. I will try to answer all your questions in order. No, I don't, it's not bad, about three inches and yes, I am drying up."

Jake thought a few seconds and said, "Do you suppose I could walk around your edge and not get muddy?"

"Well, said Oozy, 'I wouldn't exactly bet on it but I suppose it is possible."

Jake slowly inched forward and walked around Oozy. Then he sat down on the nearby grass and examined the bottom of his shoes. They didn't look *too* bad. "Maybe I'd better take them off just in case I accidentally get any closer." Jake not only took off his shoes but his socks also. He walked over to Oozy.... "I think I want to put my feet in your middle and feel how warm it is"

Oozy was pleased to share some of his warmth and said, "Come on in, Jake. It's really squishy between your toes and probably good for your feet too. You know some women put mud on their faces to make them prettier."

Jake thought that over and it sounded really smart. Sort of made sense – if mud was good for faces, it should be good for feet. He waded to the middle. Oozy had been right. It was warm and really felt good squishing up between his toes. He went to the center and it got even better. Sooooo soft…He had forgotten to roll up his jeans and the bottom of them started to soak up the muddy water. He decided that he just made his first mistake today. His Mom would see the dirty hems of his jeans and know where he had been. He knew he was going to get called Jacob Andrew and she would be mad at him so he might as well enjoy it for a few more minutes.

Oozy was happy having Jake slide around on his slippery bottom but he knew this was only for a short time. He figured that maybe the next time it rained Jake would come back and play with him.

Jake slid around for fifteen or twenty minutes and then decided he had better head for home. He stepped out of the puddle and sat back down on the grass. His Mom might not be too mad at him since his shoes hadn't gotten muddy. He put his socks on over his muddy, wet feet and then pulled his shoes on over them. Of course the <u>bottoms </u>of the shoes were still clean. It was the <u>inside</u> that had the mud and water sloshing around. The socks were soaked and of course, had soaked into his shoes. The hems of his jeans had dripped a muddy remembrance on the tops of his shoes also.

Jake said, "Oops, guess Mom won't be happy with this. Got to go, Oozy… Maybe I'll see you tomorrow and then….maybe I <u>won't</u>"

Oozy spent the rest of the sunny day quietly shrinking and thinking of Jake. By the next day Oozy was only about a third of his original size and he knew that by that day's end he would probably be all dried up.

Jacob Andrew did not get to come by the day after his wading experience. His Mom sort of chewed him out and made him stay in the yard all day. The following day he was allowed out and he went across the street to the park to see Oozy. He walked down the dirt path and came to the spot where Oozy and he had enjoyed their time together a couple of days ago. It was a dry patch. No water – no mud – and no Oozy.

He again squatted down and said softly. "Oozy, are you there somewhere?"

In a teeny, weenie voice from the ground Oozy said, "Howdy, Jake...looks like we will have to wait for a while for our next visit. I'll be watching for the rain and you to come back."

"By the time it rains again, Mom will have forgotten about this and I will come back for another visit. The next time I will be barefoot and wear shorts," whispered Jake

"That will be great, Jake. I'll be looking forward to seeing you again and maybe you can think up some new questions," answered Oozy.

Jake grinned and giggled as only a six year old can. He put his thoughts of his new friend way back in his mind to recall at a later date when it rained again...

THE MAGIC BUTTERFLY

Sami lay on her bed staring at the window where golden sunshine and a gentle summer breeze were coming in. Sighing, she watched as the white frilly curtain billowed out allowing more of the breeze to reach her. She was so alone and so unhappy. She had been without her Mommy for two years now. Daddy said Mommy had gone to live with God. She missed her so. She had no sisters or brothers, just her and Daddy in this big old house. Gertie, the housekeeper/nanny, was there during the day but she was old and quiet and was so busy doing cooking and cleaning that there never seemed to be any time to just play with her like Mommy had. Sami was to have her 5th birthday in a couple of days and not even the thought of a party gave her anything to smile about.

The doctor had told her parents there would be no more children after Sami so they had built their joy around their dark haired, happy little girl. Her Mother had become sick for a long time and then went away. Daddy tried not to cry when they spent their special times in the evenings together but their trio had certain rituals of playing that were for three and now there were just two of them. Daddy read books to her and watched videos with her and waited for them both to heal and adjust to their loss.

As she lay there staring at the fluttering curtain, a yellow butterfly with white and black wings fluttered onto the sill. It seemed to be staring at Sami. They both seemed to be in a trancelike state.

Sami thought she heard the butterfly say, "Come closer to the window so we can talk". Now even almost five year olds know that butterflies can't talk! However, Sami slid off the bed and went to the window.

"What do you want?" Sami mumbled, not expecting an answer because again even almost five year olds know that butterflies can't talk!

"I have a message for you from someone who loves you very much". Sami's eyes opened wide and her lips fell wide apart. "Someone who loved butterflies asked me to tell you that she is watching over you and to come to the sunshine where the butterflies land".

"My Mommy <u>loved</u> butterflies", Sami said excitedly.

"I believe your Mommy wants you to come out in the yard, see this beautiful day, watch the birds and butterflies that enjoy the flower garden so much.

Sami and her Mommy use to spend lots of time admiring the bright flowers and watching for the different colored butterflies float onto the pedals. "Your Mommy says if you visit the garden each and every day in the sunshine and think happy thoughts, beautiful butterflies will come and visit you and they will bring the message that your Mommy is always nearby. She will be watching you grow just like the flowers and you will be as beautiful as the little butterflies".

"But what happens when it rains and I cannot go outside because there is no sunshine and its wet? Will my Mommy be watching me then too?" Sami questioned.

The little butterfly said, "Like flowers need water to grow and butterflies need water to drink, there are sometimes that they will need to rest as you do each night. Mommy is always there – rain or shine – always watching over you and loving you".

Sami thought about all she had heard and decided to think a bit more about all this so she climbed back on the bed and stared again at the windowsill. The little butterfly flew away after a few minutes.

That night Sami ate dinner with her Daddy that Gertie had left for them. While chomping on a carrot she asked her Daddy, "Is Mommy always watching over me and can butterflies talk?" Sami knew the answer about the butterflies as kids that are almost 5 year olds KNOW that butterflies can't talk!

Her father seeing no connection between the two answered, "Yes, honey, Mommy loved you very much and will always watch over you. As for the butterflies, one has never spoken to me. Why?"

"I thought I talked with a butterfly today but maybe I was sleeping", she said uncertainly. Her father read her some stories after dinner and they watched Sponge Bob Square pants on the TV and eventually they went up to their bedrooms.

After breakfast the next day, Sami looked out the window, saw the glorious sunshine and decided she would go out and swing in the yard swing. The sun felt so warm and seemed to just warm up her whole insides as she rocked back and forth in the swing. She spotted what looked like the pretty little butterfly she saw yesterday and it was flitting from flower to flower and finally came to rest on the arm of the porch swing. "I am so happy you have come outside to see what a pretty garden it is in the daylight," the butterfly said.

"Did my Mommy send you to talk to me again? Is she nearby and watching me?" said Sami.

"Your Mommy loves you so much and it makes her smile that you have come out to play. She hopes that you will have a great time with your cousins at your birthday party and laugh a lot. She loves to see you laugh and smile. She'll watch over you and your little guests at the party."

"Will you be at my party too?" Sami asked the little butterfly.

"I will be there some of the time but I must spend a bit of time with another little girl. She is lonely too. She just moved here and doesn't know anyone yet. There is just her mother and she. As in your life, she has lost someone she loved very much, her Daddy".

"Is she a big girl or a little girl? Does she live close by or far away? If she is a little girl and lives close by, maybe she could come and play with me sometime?" Sami fired the questions rapidly.

"Yes, she is close to your age and yes, she lives close by, just a few blocks away. Maybe you will meet her one day. I need to fly away right now but your Mommy loves you every minute of every day".

Sami rubbed her eyes and came out of a dozing nap in the swing to see the little butterfly heading over the red blooms in the garden, over the green spire tree and up into the air. She watched it go as far as she could see and then it disappeared.

Steve, Sami's Daddy was on the way home from work when he remembered the note from Gertie asking him to pick up some milk. He was only a few blocks from home and was glad he remembered. He drove to Joist's Supermarket and went in. He walked quickly to the dairy products and when rounding the aisle *collided* with a young woman whose cart was piled high with grocery items. A blonde haired little *girl* was crammed in the middle of them. Some of her items fell off the pile onto the floor and Steve stopped to help pick them up, apologizing for his part in the accident.

"Do I know you?" he asked, "you look so familiar".

"So do <u>you</u>", she said.

"Are you from this area or do you go to Central Christian Church or do you work downtown somewhere near 4th and Fillmore"? Steve asked the questions as rapidly as Sami did the about the butterfly.

"The lady laughed and said, "No, I just moved here from Illinois. I haven't found a church yet for my daughter and me. I also haven't started looking for a job anywhere until we get settled in and school starts. She laughed and said, "I guess that answers all you asked but I can't talk as fast as you."

"I am originally from Illinois also… Bloomington, IL. What town do you come from"? Steve asked.

"You've <u>got</u> to be kidding! I was born in Pontiac and lived in Bloomington until just two months ago! My husband passed away over a year ago. Lindy and I moved out here a couple months ago to be near my parents who retired here in Phoenix".

"I went to Wentworth Grade School and Normal Community High School when I lived there. Is that where I know you from?" Steve asked.

"Well, I graduated from Normal Community High School in 1990", she exclaimed!

"This sure is odd – I graduated in 1987 from there", Steve said looking shocked but pleased. "You would have been a freshman when I was a junior – did you have old Peterson for history?"

"She laughed and said "Yup, who could ever forget his spitting problem when he got so excited talking about the battles in history? No one ever wanted to sit in the front row in HIS class." They both were laughing and little Lindy just smiled at her Mother's happy face. She hadn't seen it that way in a very long time.

"Do you have plans or would you like to have a cup of coffee?" Steve stammered.

"I have an hour or so before I start dinner so…yes, I would like to have coffee and talk about Bloomington and all its changes," she answered.

Steve said, "Could I meet you in about twenty minutes at the Coffee Cup across the street? I need to go home and pick up my daughter Sami first."

"Sounds great to me – Will you bring your wife along? I haven't met many people my age yet."

"I'm sorry – I didn't tell you, my wife died two years ago and there is just Sami and I".

"Oh, I am so sorry. I didn't know…please forgive me," she said quietly.

"No, you <u>didn't</u> know, so please forgive <u>me </u>for not bringing that into the conversation. There just wasn't an opportunity to talk about her and I would have told you more about our lives over the coffee", Steve said, "I will pick up Sami and bring her to the Coffee Shop in twenty minutes. She and your little girl seem about the same age. Sami needs to have a friend her age to talk to."

"So does Lindy – she hasn't met anyone yet to play with and it will do her good."

Steve grabbed the milk, paid for it and headed for the car. There was a beautiful little yellow butterfly with black and white wings sitting on his windshield wiper and it stayed there until he backed out of the parking place.

Sami was waiting excitedly as she knew it was time for her Daddy to come home. Gertie had dinner in the oven and was preparing to leave for the day. She watched out the window and finally he pulled in the driveway. He *thought* he saw the butterfly again as he put the car in park and *thought* he heard, "Be happy, Steve. I will always love you and

Sami. I want you both to smile again". He thought a moment about this but everyone knows that butterflies can't talk.

Sami ran to him and he scooped her up in his arms saying, "We are going to the Coffee Cup and you can have a dish of ice cream even <u>before</u> dinner. There is a nice little girl there about your age that is looking for a friend. She and her Mommy live a few blocks from here and I think you will really like them." He called in to Gertie and asked her to turn off the oven as they were going to be delayed for a while.

"What's her name? How old is she? Does she like to play outdoors? Does she want to come to my party?" Her Dad just couldn't keep up with Sami's questions. He said, "Hop in the car and we will go find out those answers, ok?"

Off they went toward the Coffee Cup to make new friends and renew old high school memories. They didn't know it but the little butterfly followed them for quite a ways and then soared up, up and away into the sky.